Who Was
Genghis Khan?

Who Was Genghis Khan?

By Nico Medina
Illustrated by Andrew Thomson

Grosset & Dunlap
An Imprint of Penguin Group (USA) LLC

To Jessica and Katherine,
for the Excellent Adventures—NM

To Rhia, Mum & Dad, and Dai—AT

GROSSET & DUNLAP
Published by the Penguin Group
Penguin Group (USA) LLC, 375 Hudson Street, New York, New York 10014, USA

USA | Canada | UK | Ireland | Australia | New Zealand | India | South Africa | China

penguin.com
A Penguin Random House Company

Text copyright © 2014 by Nico Medina. Illustrations copyright © 2014 by Penguin Group (USA) LLC. Cover illustration copyright © 2014 by Nancy Harrison. All rights reserved. Published by Grosset & Dunlap, a division of Penguin Young Readers Group, ʾ45 Hudson Street, New York, New York 10014. GROSSET & DUNLAP is a trademark of Penguin Group (USA) LLC. Printed in the USA.

ʾrary of Congress Cataloging-in-Publication Data is available.

ʾ260-6   10 9 8 7 6 5 4 3 2

Contents

Who Was
Genghis Khan?

The year was 1179. A teenager named Temujin slept soundly in his felt-walled tent alongside his wife, Borte.

The round tent, called a *ger*, stood alone at the edge of the steppe—a region of vast, flat grasslands in Mongolia. Temujin and Borte shared this *ger* with family and friends. Together, they formed a small clan of thirteen people.

Most clans lived close together, forming communities of thousands called tribes. But Temujin's clan lived alone and isolated.

An old woman was awakened by vibrations in the ground.

Hoofbeats. Coming closer.

She screamed for everyone to wake up.
Someone was coming!

Three hundred men on horseback from the
Merkid tribe raced toward Temujin's *ger*. Eighteen
years earlier, Temujin's father—a man named
Yesugei—had kidnapped his mother from her
Merkid husband. Now Temujin was grown, with
a wife of his own. The Merkid wanted revenge.

Temujin's clan jumped into action. But there were not enough horses for everyone to escape. In the confusion, Borte was kidnapped.

Temujin and his clan rode hard through the night. They tried to reach the safety of the forested mountains to the north. There was nowhere to hide on the treeless steppe.

For days, the Merkid searched for Temujin. Finally, they gave up and returned home with Borte as their prisoner.

Temujin climbed to the top of Burkhan Khaldun—"God mountain" in Mongolian. The Mongols worshipped the spirits of the earth, sun, and sky. Burkhan Khaldun, the tallest peak in the area, was the closest earthly place to the Eternal Blue Sky.

To thank the gods for protecting him, Temujin flicked milk into the air then sprinkled some on the ground. He prayed for guidance for three days.

Three rivers flowed from this sacred mountain, presenting Temujin with three choices. He could follow one river southeast, back toward his *ger*. But alone on the steppe, he would never be safe from future attacks. The Onon River flowed northeast, back to the forests where Temujin had grown up, barely surviving by hunting birds and mice. He did not wish to live like that again.

So Temujin chose the third river. He followed it southwest, to the Kereyid people.

The Kereyid joined forces with Temujin and his clan. They attacked the Merkid and rescued Borte.

But that was only the beginning.

Over the next twenty-seven years, Temujin would unite all the steppe tribes. He would become Genghis Khan, ruler of the Mongols, and conqueror of the largest land empire the world had ever known.

Chapter 1
Life on the Steppe

Temujin's mother, Hoelun, came from the eastern steppe. At sixteen, she married a Merkid tribesman named Chiledu. The man traveled a long way to seek her hand in marriage.

On their way back to Chiledu's homeland,

someone was watching. Yesugei was hunting
with his falcon when he spotted the couple from
atop a cliff. He thought Hoelun was beautiful.
Yesugei already had a wife, but he decided he
wanted another. He rode back to camp, returned
with his brothers, and chased after the newlyweds.

Hoelun knew they could not outrun the men.

She told Chiledu to run. If he was captured, she said, he would be killed. So Chiledu fled, and Yesugei took Hoelun to his clan.

This was life on the steppe: brutal, unforgiving, dramatic. It had been this way for centuries.

Hoelun's new life with Yesugei was different from her childhood. She grew up on the open grassland. Her people raised cows, goats, sheep, and horses for meat and milk. But Yesugei lived where the grassland met the wooded mountains. They had little livestock, and hunted in the forest for food: rodents, birds, fish—whatever they

could get.

In the spring of 1162, about a year after being kidnapped, Hoelun gave birth.

Temujin, the boy who would one day be called Genghis Khan, was born on a hill overlooking the Onon River, near the modern-day border of Mongolia and Siberia.

Yesugei had just returned from fighting the Tatar tribe in the east. He named his son after a warrior he had killed: Temujin.

Temujin grew up playing along the Onon River with his younger brothers and sister. He also had two half brothers—Begter and Belgutei.

Like all children on the steppe, Temujin grew up hunting and riding horses. By four, he could ride alone—and soon after, while standing up!

Once his legs were long enough to reach the stirrups, he shot arrows and threw lassos while riding.

When Temujin was eight or nine, his father decided to find him a wife. Together they journeyed east. Yesugei met with a man who had a daughter named Borte. She was a year older than Temujin. The fathers decided their children should marry. Temujin was to stay and work for Borte's father until it was time to marry her.

On his way back home, Yesugei saw a group of feasting Tatars. Tired and hungry, he stopped to join the party. Eight years had passed since Yesugei killed the Tatar warrior who was also named Temujin. But he was recognized, and his food was poisoned. As Yesugei rode home after the feast, he fell ill.

He sent a messenger to his son. He was dying. Temujin needed to come home.

When Temujin returned, his father was dead.

Yesugei's two widows were unimportant now. They had come from other clans. They were outsiders. Their children were too young to contribute. When the clan packed up to move to their summer home, the leader ordered his people to abandon Yesugei's family.

One person, an old man, objected. The clan leader responded by driving a spear through the old man's body. Temujin rushed to help him as everyone rode off. As the old man lay dying, Temujin sobbed. What would become of his family now?

THE MONGOLIAN STEPPE

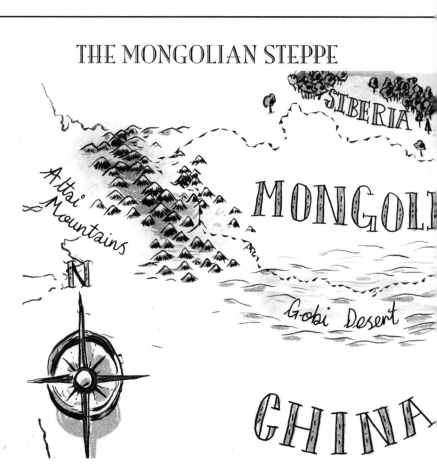

THE HIGH, TREELESS PLAINS OF MONGOLIA ARE KNOWN AS THE STEPPE. THIS ROLLING GRASSLAND COVERS AN AREA LARGER THAN TEXAS. IT IS BORDERED TO THE NORTH AND EAST BY THE FORESTS OF SIBERIA AND MANCHURIA. TO ITS WEST RISE THE SNOW-COVERED ALTAI MOUNTAINS, AND THE ARID GOBI DESERT FORMS ITS SOUTHERN BOUNDARY.

IT IS A LAND OF EXTREME WEATHER. TEMPERATURES CAN RISE TO NINETY DEGREES IN THE SUMMER, AND FALL TO FIFTY BELOW ZERO IN THE WINTER. RAINFALL IS SCARCE AND UNPREDICTABLE, SO FARMING IS NEARLY IMPOSSIBLE. BUT MELTING WINTER SNOW AND AN ABUNDANCE OF LAKES AND RIVERS MAKE IT THE PERFECT PLACE FOR RAISING LIVESTOCK.

Chapter 2
Murder and Imprisonment

Temujin's family survived by eating berries and roots. The boys made fishing hooks out of sewing needles. They made arrows from wood and bone and made clothing from the skins of mice and dogs.

Occasionally, they shared campsites with other clans. A boy named Jamuka camped alongside Temujin's family every winter. He became Temujin's best friend.

Temujin and Jamuka hunted and played together. They skated on the frozen Onon River. They threw knucklebones, small toys made from the anklebones of sheep.

When they were eleven, they gave each other special knucklebones as gifts. The next year,

they made arrowheads for each other. Then they sealed their friendship with a ceremony. By drinking a few drops of each other's blood, they became *andas*: blood brothers.

One winter, Jamuka did not return. Would the blood brothers ever meet again?

In steppe society, when no father was present, the oldest male in the family was in charge. In Temujin's family, that was his older half brother, Begter. Begter picked on Temujin. Once, he stole a fish Temujin had caught just to show Temujin who was in charge.

But Temujin, now twelve or thirteen years old, wanted to be the boss. He decided to kill Begter.

One day, Temujin and his younger brother, Khasar, approached Begter. Khasar was better with a bow and arrow, so he stood in front of Begter. Temujin aimed his arrow at Begter's back.

Begter knew he had been defeated. He knelt down to surrender and asked that Temujin let his younger brother, Belgutei, live. Temujin agreed.

And with that, Temujin and Khasar shot their arrows and left Begter to bleed to death.

Hoelun became angry. She called her sons murderers, animals, monsters. She told Temujin that his only companion now would be his shadow.

Word of Temujin's actions traveled to his father's tribe that had abandoned him years earlier. They rode to Temujin's camp to punish him. Temujin hid but was soon discovered. A yoke—a wooden bar used to harness animals—was placed over his neck, and he was taken to their camp as a prisoner.

Every day, he was moved to a different *ger*, where he would be guarded by a servant. One day, while his captors were celebrating a festival, Temujin made a break for it. He swung his yoke, knocking out the boy guarding him.

Temujin ran to the river and hid in a clump of weeds. He was spotted by a man who told

Temujin to remain there until dark, then run
home.

Instead, Temujin ran to the man's *ger* at
nightfall. The man was angry at Temujin for
putting his family in danger. But there was
something special about Temujin, a fire in his
eyes. The man wanted to help.

He removed Temujin's yoke. The next day, the family hid Temujin in a cart of wool. At night, they gave him food and a horse. Temujin was grateful. His own clan had left his family for dead on the steppe. Years later they returned, only to imprison him. But a poor family with everything to lose had risked their lives to help him.

On the steppe, clan and tribe meant everything. But for Temujin, they had meant nothing but pain and suffering. The family Temujin made—like his *anda*, Jamuka—and the decency of strangers were what he placed his faith in.

Chapter 3
Friends and Allies

When Temujin was sixteen years old, he traveled back across the steppe to claim his bride. Borte's family was happy to see him. Her father gave the couple a valuable coat made of black sable fur as a wedding gift.

Temujin returned home with Borte, eager
to start a family. But he could not risk being
captured again—or worse, killed. To protect his
clan, he needed allies.

Temujin visited the powerful Kereyid tribe
seeking an alliance. He met with their leader,
Toghril, in his golden *ger*. Since Toghril and
Temujin's father had been *andas*, Temujin hoped
Toghril would agree to become his ally. To seal
the deal, he gave Toghril the beautiful sable coat.

THE NOMADIC TRIBES OF THE STEPPE

MANY PEOPLE CALLED THE STEPPE HOME.
TEMUJIN'S TRIBE, THE MONGOLS, WERE NOT
UNIFIED, BUT DIVIDED INTO SEPARATE CLANS. MORE
POWERFUL TRIBES SURROUNDED THEM. TO THEIR
NORTHWEST WERE THE MERKID, WHO SOMETIMES
RODE ON REINDEER. THE TRIBES TO THEIR
SOUTHWEST AND FAR WEST WERE THE KEREYID
AND THE NAIMAN. TO THE EAST WERE THE TATARS.

THE TRIBES WERE NOMADIC, MEANING THEY DID
NOT HAVE PERMANENT SETTLEMENTS. THEY MOVED
WITH THE SEASONS IN SEARCH OF GRAZING LANDS
FOR THEIR HERDS OF SHEEP, GOATS, COWS, AND
HORSES.

THEY WERE POOR. BECAUSE THERE WAS VERY
LITTLE TRADE WITH FOREIGN COUNTRIES, IT
WAS EASIER TO JUST ATTACK A NEIGHBOR AND
STEAL THINGS. YEAR AFTER YEAR, CENTURY AFTER
CENTURY, THE STEPPE TRIBES ATTACKED AND
RAIDED OTHER CLANS AND TRIBES.

Toghril accepted Temujin's gift and offered him a position of power within the Kereyid tribe. But Temujin declined. He only wanted Toghril's protection. In return, he and his men would fight for Toghril whenever it was needed. Temujin returned home.

One day, eight of Temujin's horses were stolen. He rode his only remaining horse to pursue the thieves. On his journey he met a boy named Boorchu who helped find and recover the horses.

Temujin asked Boorchu how many horses he would like as a reward, but Boorchu refused. "I joined you," Boorchu said, "because I saw that you were in trouble and in need of help." Then Boorchu joined Temujin's camp. The two became lifelong friends.

Around this time, another boy named Jelme joined Temujin's camp. Although Jelme was sent to Temujin as a servant, he was treated as an equal. One day, Jelme would become Temujin's most trusted commander.

Temujin now had powerful protection and new friends in his clan.

But he still had enemies.

It was around this time that the Merkid raided Temujin's camp and kidnapped Borte.

After praying for guidance on Burkhan Khaldun, Temujin rode down the mountain to ask his Kereyid allies for help. Toghril offered twenty thousand of his troops, plus twenty thousand more from another ally.

That ally was Temujin's blood brother. His *anda*, Jamuka. The blood brothers were reunited!

The men rode over the mountains to attack the Merkid camp and rescue Borte.

But Borte did not know the attack was a rescue mission. When the Merkid scattered, she fled.

Only after Borte heard Temujin calling her name did she turn and run into his arms.

After looting the Merkid camp, everyone returned home.

Temujin's clan joined with Jamuka's. Borte was pregnant and in 1179 gave birth to a son.

Temujin named him Jochi, which means "visitor" or "guest." Perhaps he gave him this name because they were guests in Jamuka's clan. Or perhaps he felt Jochi was a merely a visitor to the Mongol tribe. Some say Jochi's father was not actually Temujin, but a member of the Merkid. Whatever the reason, Temujin raised Jochi as his own son.

Life was good for Temujin. He had a wife, a son, close friends, powerful allies, and a tribe.

Temujin and Jamuka sealed their friendship in front of Jamuka's tribe by exchanging gifts from the Merkid raid: golden sashes and strong horses. After a celebratory feast, the two slept beside each other under one blanket, as real brothers did.

But the good times would not last.

Chapter 4
Power Struggle

Jamuka's people were animal herders, not lowly hunters like Temujin. They

lived on the open grassland where their sheep, goats, and other livestock could graze. For the first time, Temujin's people enjoyed a steady diet of milk, cheese, and meat. They grew strong, and they were truly part of a tribe.

Jamuka wanted to unite all the warring Mongol clans of the steppe into one, powerful tribe. Temujin wanted the same thing.

As Jamuka's *anda*, Temujin enjoyed a position of power within the clan. He was always at Jamuka's side, helping him and learning from him.

But after a year and a half, Jamuka began treating Temujin more like a little brother than an equal. One night, he told Temujin to camp alongside the river, where the sheep and goats could graze. Jamuka would camp on the steppe with the horses, cows, and camels. This was an insult.

Borte became angry. She told Temujin that Jamuka had grown tired of them. They should leave Jamuka's tribe. Whoever else wished to leave could join them.

That's just what Temujin did.

One night when Jamuka stopped to camp,

Temujin's group kept moving. Some people deserted Jamuka to go with them. They marched all night.

Jamuka did not pursue Temujin, but over the next two decades, the two became bitter enemies.

Over the years, Temujin gained more followers, and three more sons: Chaghatai, Ogodei, and Tolui.

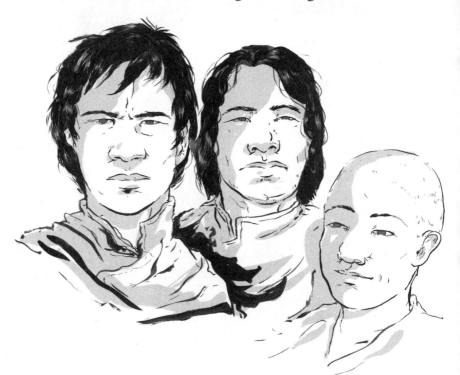

Unlike other tribal leaders, Temujin rewarded positions of power to men based on their ability rather than their family ties. His servant Jelme and friend Boorchu became close advisers. His younger brother Khasar was in charge of security.

One summer day in 1189, Temujin summoned his followers to a meeting at Blue Lake. Here, he was named the leader of the Mongols. But Jamuka still had many followers of his own.

Temujin sent word to his powerful ally, Toghril. He promised that he was not going to challenge Toghril's authority. He wished only to unite the Mongols under one leader, and that the Mongols would remain subservient to the Kereyid. Toghril was pleased that someone was challenging Jamuka's growing power.

Jamuka became angry at this news. He attacked Temujin's camp. Temujin and his men escaped to the mountains. While they hid, Jamuka returned to Temujin's camp.

Mongols had always preferred to hunt and fight by shooting arrows from far away. They avoided hand-to-hand combat whenever possible. But Jamuka beheaded one of Temujin's followers and tied the head to the tail of a horse.

Then, he boiled seventy of Temujin's followers
alive.

To the Mongols, the head was the most sacred
part of the body, and the spilling of blood was a
grave offense. Boiling a man killed his soul as well
as his body. After these gruesome incidents, many
deserted Jamuka in favor of Temujin.

Temujin and his men recovered from
the attack. Five years later, in 1195, a great

opportunity arose when Toghril asked Temujin to help raid the Tatars of the eastern steppe. There was much treasure to be had.

The vast and wealthy Jurched Empire lay south of the Gobi Desert, in northern China. Fifty million people lived there, and they called their leader the Golden Khan. Toghril had been asked by the leader of the Jurched people to attack the Tatars.

For years, the Tatars had protected the Jurched from other steppe tribes. In return, the Jurched provided the Tatars luxury goods like silk, iron weapons, and jewelry. But now the Golden Khan worried that the Tatars had become too powerful. He feared the Tatars might one day attack his people, so he decided to attack them first.

Temujin was happy to help. The Tatars had poisoned his father—and on the steppe, it was never too late for revenge.

The battle was decisive. The Tatars were beaten. Temujin returned home rich with loot.

Satin clothing threaded with gold, a cradle embossed with silver, blankets made of silk. His people had never seen such luxury!

From then on Temujin sought to expand his own territory. A tribe to his south had promised to help him fight the Tatars. But they had never shown up. Instead, while Temujin was away, they'd raided his camp.

In 1197, Temujin decided to attack and raid this tribe in revenge. The tribe's leaders were beheaded for betraying him. But rather than take everyone else as prisoners or slaves—as was common on the steppe—he welcomed them into his tribe. This was a new way for a leader to behave.

By unifying the two tribes, Temujin's tribe grew bigger than ever. Temujin moved his people onto the newly conquered land. With wide-open grazing lands, it was the perfect place to settle. It was also near a natural spring, so they called their new home Aurag, Mongolian for *source*.

Four years later, in 1201, Jamuka summoned his own followers to a meeting. There, he was named Gur-Khan, "khan of all khans." This was a direct challenge to Temujin.

The men who were once as close as brothers faced off in battle. But Jamuka realized he was outnumbered and fled.

During the fight, Temujin had been shot in the neck by an arrow. It may have been tipped with poison, because as the battle died down for the night, Temujin lost consciousness. His faithful friend and servant Jelme sucked blood from the wound for hours. When Temujin awoke and asked for a drink, Jelme snuck across the battlefield and brought back some yogurt. Temujin survived, and he never forgot Jelme's devotion.

The next day, Temujin chased down and captured all his enemies who had snuck away during the night. Once again, he had the leaders executed and accepted the rest of the tribe into his own.

Jamuka had escaped.

The final showdown between the blood brothers would have to wait.

Chapter 5
Temujin's Tribe, Temujin's Rules

For centuries, steppe warfare revolved around one thing: looting. One tribe attacked another, and if the victims fled, the battle was over and the victors took all the losers' belongings.

In 1202, at the request of Toghril, forty-year-old Temujin returned to fight the Tatars. Before the battle, Temujin made some new rules: First, the battle would go on until the enemy was defeated once and for all. Second, any looted property would go directly to Temujin. As leader, he would divide the goods as he saw fit. Finally, Temujin decreed that if a man died in battle, his family would receive his fair share of the loot.

Steppe life had never been fair, and these new laws were revolutionary. Still, some men did not like the new rules and deserted Temujin to join Jamuka. Those who stayed were all the more loyal. Had these laws been in place when Temujin was a boy, his family might never have been abandoned by their tribe.

Temujin led his Mongol army into battle and this time defeated the Tatars for good. Temujin distributed the winnings evenly, gaining the trust and respect of his people.

However, this new method of warfare
presented Temujin with a problem. Because he did
not allow the Tatars to flee, he now had thousands
of new captives. If he let them live, they would
grow stronger, and they would be at war again in
a few years.

Temujin and the tribal leaders decided to execute any Tatar male taller than the axle of a wheel. Every Tatar man, and many Tatar boys, would be killed. Everyone else would become part of the Mongol tribe.

It was a brutal decision. The Tatars were all Mongols now.

Temujin had to make sure all members of his tribe obeyed him, and only him. To do this, he reorganized his army. He formed squads of ten soldiers each. The soldiers in a squad came from different tribes but fought together as brothers.

They were forbidden from leaving behind their comrades in battle. The oldest man in each squad was the leader.

Ten squads formed a company of one hundred soldiers. Ten companies formed a battalion of a thousand men. Company and battalion leaders were selected by the soldiers. Finally, ten companies formed a *tumen* of ten thousand soldiers. Temujin personally selected the leader of each *tumen*.

Now, when Temujin gave an order, it traveled easily from the top down.

Temujin had absorbed many thousands of people into his tribe. Now he proposed to Toghril that his first son, Jochi, marry Toghril's daughter. Toghril was an old man by now. Some said Temujin wished to bring the Kereyid under his command once Toghril died.

At first, Toghril refused Temujin's offer.
Then, perhaps fearful of Temujin's response, he
reconsidered. After all, Temujin commanded an
army of eighty thousand soldiers. Toghril sent
word to Temujin,
accepting his offer
and setting a date
for the wedding.

But Toghril
had a dirty trick
up his sleeve. He
assembled a group
of men to meet
Temujin and his
family on the
steppe. It was not
a welcoming party.
They had been sent
to murder them.

Chapter 6
The Final Showdown

Temujin was warned by a shepherd of the planned sneak attack. His party scattered and Toghril's men gave chase. Eventually, Temujin and nineteen of his men arrived on the muddy shores of Lake Baljuna. They came from nine different tribes. They included Christians, Buddhists, and Muslims. Some, like Temujin, worshipped the Eternal Blue Sky.

The men were low on food. When a wild horse appeared, the men took it as a positive sign. Temujin's brother, Khasar, captured and killed the horse, and the men ate it. They drank muddy water from the lake and pledged their eternal allegiance to Temujin. They would not be defeated so easily.

Temujin sent messengers to tell his soldiers to march toward Toghril's troops. Horse stations were established all along the route. When Temujin and his men left Lake Baljuna, they rode their horses as fast as they could. When their horses tired, fresh horses were waiting for them at the horse stations. Temujin called this the "lightning advance," because of how quickly he and his men traveled.

Toghril, thinking Temujin was days away, did not expect the attack so soon. Victory was swift for Temujin. Toghril tried to escape and was killed.

Temujin continued on to the western steppe. There he would fight the Naiman tribe—who had allied with Jamuka—for control of the entire steppe.

Temujin was greatly outnumbered. The night before the battle, Temujin told each of his men to light five fires. This would make his army appear much larger than it really was. Before sunrise, he ordered some of his men to attack in small groups in a "tumbleweed formation." Squads quietly approached the enemy, then spread

out and shot arrows from different positions. Before the enemy could fire back, Temujin's men scattered again. This confused the enemy.

When daylight broke, Temujin's soldiers formed lines of men standing side by side. The first line of men shot arrows at the Naiman troops, then made way for the next line of men with another round of arrows. This was called the "lake formation," because the men were like the waves of a lake—as soon as one line of soldiers disappeared, another stepped forward to take their place.

In response, the Naiman spread their defense into a long, thin line. Now, Temujin reorganized his troops into the triangle-shaped "chisel formation," which penetrated deep into the enemy lines.

The Naiman had been outsmarted and outfought. On one moonless night, many tried to escape. Without the moonlight, they could not see and fell into a deep gorge. The few remaining

Naiman soldiers were defeated the next morning.

Jamuka and a small band of his followers escaped to the forest. For a year, they wandered, hunting and eating wild animals, just like Temujin had as a boy. Eventually, Jamuka's men grew tired and turned him in. For their disloyalty, Temujin had them executed.

Temujin gave Jamuka one last chance to put their past behind them and to live as *andas* once again. "Surely, in the days of killing and being killed, the pit of your stomach and your heart pained for me," he said.

But Jamuka said that he would be a better friend to Temujin in death. He told his blood brother: "Kill me and lay down my dead bones in the high ground." From there, he could watch over Temujin and his people forever.

Temujin granted Jamuka's wish and ordered his execution. His *anda* was dead.

And Temujin, now forty-three years old, was the undisputed ruler of the steppe.

Chapter 7
Temujin Becomes Genghis Khan

One year later, in 1206, Temujin summoned a meeting near his childhood home along the Onon River. Thousands attended. Lines of *gers* stretched for miles in every direction.

In the shadow of Burkhan Khaldun, the united tribes of the steppe officially proclaimed Temujin their leader. He was given the name Chinggis Khan. In Mongolian, *chin* means strong or fearless, and *chino* means wolf. *Khan* means ruler.

Today, he is known more commonly by another name: Genghis Khan.

There were days of celebrations. There was feasting and music. Men competed in horse racing, wrestling, and archery. Shamans beat their drums and chanted to the nature spirits and the Eternal Blue Sky.

WHAT DID GENGHIS KHAN
LOOK LIKE?

BECAUSE HE WOULDN'T ALLOW ANYONE TO
PAINT HIS PORTRAIT, NO ONE KNOWS WHAT
GENGHIS KHAN REALLY LOOKED LIKE. ALL
PAINTINGS OF GENGHIS KHAN WERE MADE AFTER
HIS DEATH.

ONE PERSIAN CHRONICLER DESCRIBED HIM AS
TALL AND VIGOROUS, WITH SPARKLING CAT'S EYES.
A CHINESE SCHOLAR SAID HE HAD A WIDE BROW
AND A LONG BEARD. SOME SAY HE HAD RED HAIR
AND DARK GREEN OR GRAY EYES. BUT NO ONE IS
CERTAIN.

Genghis Khan gave his people a new name: the Great Mongol Nation. Their nation was huge. One million people (and up to twenty million animals!) called it home.

He imposed a new set of rules—the Great Law of Genghis Khan—to keep peace and maintain order. The different tribes could keep their local customs and laws, as long as they followed the Great Law.

Under the Great Law, every man between fifteen and seventy had to fight in the army. Stealing and kidnapping were forbidden. Enslavement of any Mongol was illegal. Stealing livestock was punishable by death. A "lost and  found" program was started for animals found on the steppe. An official hunting season was established in the fall and winter, so baby animals could grow in the spring and summer.

He also established mail service. The military provided horses and riders to deliver messages from one postal station to the next. The stations were set up about every twenty miles, and they were run by local families. As the Mongol empire grew, the postal service grew with it.

Finally, under the Great Law, freedom of religion was guaranteed. Everyone in the Great Mongol Nation could worship freely without harm.

At this time, no Mongol could read or write. To record his Great Law, Genghis Khan established a written language for his people.

In 1207, one year after being named Genghis

Khan, the Mongol leader sent Jochi and a *tumen* of ten thousand soldiers north, to Siberia. There, Jochi made alliances with the forest tribes. He returned home with new recruits for the Mongol army and products such as fur, lumber, and hunting birds.

Genghis Khan was happy to receive the men and goods. But the riches he sought were on the *other* side of the Gobi Desert in the wealthy Jurched Empire of northern China. Fifty million farmers and city dwellers called the Jurched Empire home. Behind their heavily guarded city walls lay treasures in gold, silver, pearls, silk, satin, and metal.

With the most powerful and disciplined army in the world at his back, Genghis Khan set his sights on China.

Chapter 8
The Invasion of China

In 1210, the Golden Khan, ruler of the Jurched Empire, died. The new Golden Khan, his son, sent an ambassador to meet with Genghis Khan.

To the Jurched people of China, the Mongols were nothing but a raggedy band of nomads. The Jurched representative demanded that Genghis Khan bow to the power of the great Golden Khan.

If Genghis Khan was lucky, perhaps the Golden Khan would give him a meager bit of treasure in exchange for his loyalty and military service.

But Genghis Khan would bow to no man.

Instead, he cursed the Golden Khan's name and spit in the direction of China. Then he jumped on his horse and galloped off.

This was a declaration of war. Genghis Khan knew it.

In the spring of 1211, he summoned his people. The Mongols separated themselves into men, women, and children to pray for guidance. After three days at the top of Burkhan Khaldun, Genghis Khan came down from the mountain and announced to his people: "The Eternal Blue Sky has promised us victory and vengeance."

That May, 65,000 Mongol soldiers left for China, crossing the six-hundred-mile-wide Gobi Desert in just one month. When they arrived, they began terrorizing the countryside, burning villages and destroying crops.

Peasants fled to the Jurched's walled cities for protection, clogging the roads.

THE MONGOL WAR MACHINE

GOING TO WAR TOOK A GREAT DEAL OF EFFORT. BUT THE MONGOLS THOUGHT OF EVERYTHING.

SCOUTS WENT AHEAD OF THE ARMY TO CHECK FOR WATER SOURCES, ROUGH TERRAIN, GRAZING LAND, AND HUMAN SETTLEMENTS. ONCE A ROUTE WAS CHOSEN, THE ARMY LEFT.

EACH MAN CARRIED ONLY WHAT HE NEEDED— FLINTS TO START FIRES, SEWING NEEDLES, DRIED MEAT AND MILK PASTE, CANTEENS, LASSOS, AND ARROWS. BECAUSE OF THIS, THERE WAS NO NEED FOR A SLOW-MOVING SUPPLY TRAIN, VULNERABLE TO ATTACK.

BUT THE MONGOL ARMY WAS NOTHING WITHOUT THEIR HORSES. THEY TRAVELED ENTIRELY ON HORSEBACK, SWIFTLY AND EFFICIENTLY. EXTRA HORSES WERE BROUGHT TO BE MILKED, EATEN, OR RIDDEN WHEN OTHER HORSES GREW TIRED. IF THE MEN RAN OUT OF WATER, THEY DRANK HORSES' BLOOD.

SOLDIERS FOLLOWED THE INSTRUCTIONS OF THEIR COMMANDERS TO A FAULT. THEIR LOYALTY AND SELF-SUFFICIENCY MADE THEM AN UNSTOPPABLE FORCE.

The cities overflowed with refugees. With too many mouths to feed and the crops destroyed, food became scarce. People starved to death.

The Mongols used many methods to attack the Jurched cities. They enslaved Jurched engineers and had them build catapults, which threw stones or vats of boiling liquid at the walls.

They dammed rivers to flood the cities. They built oversize bows called ballistas that shot large arrows that could break through walls.

Trickery worked, too. In the "dogfight" tactic, the Mongols purposefully dropped their supplies and rode away. To the Jurched, this looked like the Mongols had retreated. The city gates were opened and the Jurched emerged to collect the supplies the Mongols had "dropped." The Mongols quickly raced back and entered the city.

The great Jurched cities fell—Shenyang, Shandong, Hebei, Shanxi. The Jurched surrendered. The Golden Khan pledged submission to Genghis Khan and promised to send him treasure every year as tribute.

But as soon as Genghis Khan left the Jurched capital of Zhongdu, the Golden Khan fled, moving his capital south to the city of Kaifeng. The Mongols returned and looted Zhongdu for a month.

They set fires throughout the city. Thousands
died. When Genghis Khan left *this* time, an army
stayed behind to guard the city.

The Jurched lands and cities became part of
the growing Mongol empire. Eventually, even the
new capital of Kaifeng fell to Mongol troops.

Chapter 9
A Whole New World

In the spring of 1215, the Mongols were treated to a dazzling sight when their soldiers returned from China. Seemingly endless caravans of camels and oxcarts poured onto the steppe, loaded with more treasure than anyone had thought possible.

Rugs and blankets. Wall hangings and cushions. There was so much silk, it was used as packing material. Cords of silk were twisted together to make rope. The silks came in more colors than the Mongols even knew existed.

Barrels of wine, honey, and black tea. Porcelain bowls, bronze knives, and iron weapons. Metal stirrups for the  Mongols' warhorses. Beautiful furniture for their felt-walled *gers*. Jewelry made from precious stones, pearls, and coral. Perfumes and makeup. Board games and wooden puppets.

The world's riches flowed onto the remote steppe of the Great Mongol Nation. There was so much loot that buildings had to be constructed to store everything.

Thousands of captured people followed the bountiful caravans. Acrobats, magicians, jugglers, and musicians. Doctors and pharmacists. Artists, writers, and translators. These people were the Mongols' "human treasure," and although they were servants, they were treated well.

Genghis Khan divided the loot among the Mongols. His people had never known such comfort and luxury.

But all this came at a price. Over the next few years, the Mongols got used to "the good life." They wanted more, and different, luxury goods. Their "human treasure" also needed to be fed and housed. Craftsmen required raw materials such as wood, gold, and clay.

Genghis Khan had fought for years to unite the steppe tribes in peace. Now he had new responsibilities. He decided to expand trade with the wealthy Muslim empire of Khwarizm.

But first, he had to decide who would rule the empire when he died.

Chapter 10
Deciding a Successor

In 1219, Genghis Khan was an old man at fifty-seven, and he had an important decision to make. Genghis Khan summoned his four sons.

He wanted to hear what they thought. He told
his oldest son, Jochi, to speak first. By choosing
Jochi to go first, it seemed like Genghis Khan was
indicating who he believed should be ruler.

His second son, Chaghatai, exploded. He
wanted to know how his father could pick Jochi,
when Jochi did not share his father's blood. Jochi,
he said, was the son of the Merkid tribesman who
had kidnapped their mother, Borte, decades earlier.

The two brothers fought.

Genghis Khan told Chaghatai that by insulting Jochi, he insulted their mother. He reminded them how hard it had been to form the Great Mongol Nation. He spoke of what life was like when everyone was fighting one another.

Genghis Khan now knew that if he left the empire in the hands of either brother, there would be civil war. He decided that his third son, Ogodei, would rule the empire as Great Khan. Jochi and Chaghatai would be given different sections of the empire. This would keep them separated. The youngest son, Tolui, would be left in charge of the old homeland on the Onon River.

Relieved to have his successor decided, Genghis Khan turned back to the growing needs of his people. The Khwarizm Empire was beckoning.

THE SECRET HISTORY OF THE MONGOLS

MUCH OF WHAT WE KNOW ABOUT THE LIFE OF GENGHIS KHAN COMES FROM A BOOK CALLED *THE SECRET HISTORY OF THE MONGOLS*. THE BOOK CHRONICLES GENGHIS KHAN'S LIFE, FROM BEGINNING TO END. WHAT MAKES THIS BOOK SO "SECRETIVE" IS THAT NO ONE IS CERTAIN WHO WROTE IT.

NOT LONG AFTER THE BOOK WAS FINISHED, EVERY COPY OF IT DISAPPEARED. BY THE 1400S, THE ONLY COPIES LEFT WERE CHINESE TRANSLATIONS. FOR MORE THAN FOUR CENTURIES, *THE SECRET HISTORY* REMAINED HIDDEN TO THE WESTERN WORLD.

IN 1866, A RUSSIAN MONK DISCOVERED A COPY AND TRANSLATED IT. IT WAS THEN TRANSLATED INTO MODERN MONGOLIAN IN 1917. MANY MORE TRANSLATIONS EXIST TODAY. A GOLD-PLATED COPY IS DISPLAYED IN THE MODERN MONGOLIAN CAPITOL BUILDING IN ULAANBAATAR, AND ALMOST EVERY MONGOLIAN FAMILY HAS A COPY IN THEIR HOME.

Chapter 11
From the Rising Sun to the Setting Sun

Genghis Khan had more goods from China than he knew what to do with. The Mongol people were well fed and comfortable. They had grown accustomed to the silks and jewels that had once seemed so exotic.

To the Mongols' west lay the Khwarizm Empire (present-day Iran, Afghanistan, Turkmenistan, Uzbekistan, and beyond). Khwarizm was a young and large empire. It was just twelve years older than the Great Mongol Nation and stretched more than 1,500 miles across. People in Khwarizm knew the secrets of glassmaking. They were skilled at working with steel, farming cotton fields, and weaving beautiful textiles.

Genghis Khan sent word
to the leader of Khwarizm,
Sultan Muhammad II.
He told the sultan he
did not wish to expand
his Mongol empire.
He wished only for a
peaceful trading partnership
with Khwarizm. Genghis
Khan referred to himself
as the ruler of the lands

**SULTAN
MUHAMMAD II**

of the rising sun, and called the sultan ruler of the
lands of the setting sun.

The sultan considered the Mongols uncivilized.
He did not want them coming to his lands. But
he wasn't ready to fight their powerful army, so
he agreed to trade. In the meantime, he secretly
prepared for war.

In 1219, Genghis Khan sent a caravan of 450
merchants to the city of Otrar, in what is now

southern Kazakhstan. They had camel cloth, jade, and silver to sell and trade. The governor of Otrar called the merchants spies and had them executed.

Genghis Khan sent a group of men to the sultan to demand an apology. He wanted harsh punishment for the murderous governor of Otrar.

In response, Sultan Muhammad II killed some of the ambassadors! He cut the faces of those he'd spared to send a message to Genghis Khan.

When word reached Genghis Khan, he became furious. He climbed his sacred mountain and prayed to the Eternal Blue Sky: "Grant me strength to exact vengeance."

Genghis Khan and his sons galloped to
Khwarizm with more than 100,000 soldiers.
Their first stop was Otrar. It took months to
overtake the city, but the Mongols were finally
victorious. They executed the governor.

The army next approached the city of Bukhara
from the forbidding
Red Desert.

Merchants traveled hundreds of miles out of their way to avoid this harsh landscape. But Genghis Khan crossed in the cold winter months, when dew formed on the ground and short grasses grew for his horses. He befriended desert nomads who helped show him the best way to Bukhara.

By the end of 1220, all the cities of Khwarizm had fallen to the Mongol armies. The sultan escaped to an island in the Caspian Sea, where he later died.

Genghis Khan had only wished to trade with Khwarizm. Because of his violent expansion into China, however, the sultan did not trust him. It seemed Genghis Khan now had only enemies and subjects.

The Mongol Empire stretched three thousand miles across. Genghis Khan, now more than sixty years old, ruled the land from the rising sun in the east to the setting sun in the west.

In the winter of 1226, Genghis Khan left

home once again to put down a rebellion in northwest China. While crossing the Gobi Desert, he stopped to hunt wild horses. During the hunt, the horse he was riding got spooked and threw him to the ground. The old man suffered serious internal injuries.

Genghis Khan soon developed a high fever, but he refused to quit. He rode on across the desert with his troops. Six months later, Genghis Khan died at camp in his felt-walled tent. Just days later, his sad and angry troops killed everyone in the rebellious city. Then Genghis Khan's body was loaded onto a cart and returned home.

PROPAGANDA

AT THE TIME OF THE MONGOL INVASION, THE MUSLIMS OF KHWARIZM WERE THE RICHEST AND MOST SOPHISTICATED PEOPLE IN THE WORLD. THEY STUDIED ASTRONOMY AND MATHEMATICS AND WERE HIGHLY LITERATE.

GENGHIS KHAN USED THIS TO HIS ADVANTAGE. HE HAD SCRIBES WRITE STORIES ABOUT THE DREADED MONGOLS AND THEIR BLOODY ATTACKS.

IN THESE ACCOUNTS, THE VIOLENCE WAS GREATLY
EXAGGERATED. THESE STORIES, ALSO KNOWN AS
PROPAGANDA, SPREAD THROUGHOUT KHWARIZM,
AND EVEN AS FAR AS EUROPE.

GENGHIS KHAN WAS CLEVER AND ORGANIZED
ENOUGH TO SPREAD FEAR TO PARTS OF THE WORLD
HE HAD YET TO CONQUER. THIS ALLOWED HIM TO
USE PROPAGANDA—IN THIS CASE, HIS REPUTATION
AS A FEARSOME WARLORD—TO WORK FOR HIM.
GENGHIS KHAN ALWAYS PREFERRED TO HAVE A
CITY SURRENDER BEFORE IT WAS ATTACKED.

The Mongols wanted to keep Genghis Khan's final resting place a secret. According to legend, everyone who saw the forty-day funeral procession was killed. After burying their leader, eight hundred horsemen trampled the ground surrounding the grave, so no one could tell where he was buried. The legend also says that the horsemen were killed, then the men who killed them were also killed.

For fifty years, the sons and grandsons of
Genghis Khan expanded the Mongol Empire.
At its height, it covered nearly one-quarter of the
Earth's land. The Khans ruled as far south as
Vietnam. Their armies conquered Baghdad, the
largest and richest city in the Muslim world, then
continued to Syria and Turkey. They galloped
across the Eurasian plain into Russia, Ukraine,
and Hungary. European knights, in their clunky
metal armor, were no match for the swift and
fearless Mongol troops.

THE GREAT TABOO

THE 150-SQUARE-MILE AREA SURROUNDING
GENGHIS KHAN'S BURIAL SITE WAS CLOSED TO
OUTSIDERS FOR NEARLY EIGHT HUNDRED YEARS.
ELITE SOLDIERS GUARDED THE AREA, ALLOWING
ONLY DIRECT DESCENDANTS OF GENGHIS KHAN TO
ENTER—AND ONLY FOR FAMILY FUNERALS. THE AREA
IS KNOWN AS *IKH KHORIG*, OR THE GREAT TABOO.
   WHEN MONGOLIA CAME UNDER SOVIET
CONTROL IN 1924, THE GOVERNMENT IN MOSCOW
REPLACED THE MONGOLIAN GUARDS WITH TANKS.

THEY DID NOT WANT GENGHIS KHAN'S GRAVE TO
BECOME A PLACE FOR THE MONGOLIAN PEOPLE
TO GATHER, AND THEY RENAMED IT SIMPLY "HIGHLY
RESTRICTED AREA." THEY THEN SURROUNDED IT
WITH AN EVEN LARGER "RESTRICTED AREA." ROADS
WERE BUILT TO THE FORBIDDEN ZONE, BUT NEVER
WITHIN ITS BOUNDARIES.

    IT WAS NOT UNTIL 1989 THAT ARCHAEOLOGISTS
AND OUTSIDERS WERE ALLOWED TO ENTER THE
GREAT TABOO.

Genghis Khan and his heirs terrorized and murdered millions of innocent people. They destroyed cities and turned rich farmland into pastures. But under their rule, ideas and technology from all over the globe were shared freely. Roads, bridges, and tens of thousands of schools were built. Manufacturing and trade flourished. Mongol ambassadors traveled as far as France and England. Holy men from the world's great religions were invited to debate one another before the Mongol court.

Today, Mongolians look back on Genghis Khan as a great leader. He is the father of their nation. He put an end to internal squabbling and brought peace and prosperity to the harsh and isolated steppe. His image appears on stamps, money, and even chocolate bars.

Though the site of his grave still remains
unknown, many believe Genghis Khan was laid to
rest where he so often knelt before the Eternal Blue
Sky. Rising high above the steppe, atop his most
sacred mountain, Burkhan Khaldun.

TIMELINE OF GENGHIS KHAN'S LIFE

1162	Born on a hill near the Onon River
1171	Father is poisoned by Tatars and dies; family is abandoned by his father's tribe
1173	Becomes blood brothers with Jamuka
1175	Murders his half brother, Begter, then is kidnapped and imprisoned by his former tribe
1178	Marries Borte and forges an alliance with the Kereyid ruler, Toghril
1179	Borte is kidnapped by the Merkid, then rescued by Temujin, Jamuka, and Toghril Joins Jamuka's tribe First son, Jochi, is born
1181	Leaves Jamuka's tribe
1189	Named leader of the Mongols at Blue Lake
1190	Fights first battle against Jamuka
1195	Raids the Tatars
1197	Establishes Aurag, a homeland for his people
1201	Battles Jamuka's forces a second time, with the help of Toghril
1202	Conquers the Tatars; reorganizes the Mongol army
1204	Defeats Jamuka
1206	Is named Genghis Khan; establishes the Great Mongol Nation
1211	Attacks the Jurched in northern China
1219	Names Ogodei, his third son, as his successor
1220	Conquers the Khwarizm Empire
1227	Dies while on campaign in northwest China

TIMELINE OF THE WORLD

King Suryavarman II, builder of Angkor Wat in Cambodia, dies	CA. 1150
Henry II becomes King of England	1154
The Jurched navy of northern China is defeated by the Sung of southern China	1161
Construction begins on Notre Dame cathedral in Paris	1163
Thomas Becket, Archbishop of Canterbury, is murdered	1170
Work begins on the Tower of Pisa	1173
The Tower of Pisa begins to lean	1178
The Genpei War in Japan begins between the rival Taira and Minamoto clans	1180
St. Francis of Assisi is born	1181
European leaders launch the Third Crusade to take back the Holy Land from the Muslims	1189
Arabic numerals are introduced to Europe	1202
Dunama Dabbalemi becomes king of the Kanem Empire in present-day Chad	1203
Constantinople, capital of the Byzantine Empire, is captured in the Fourth Crusade	1204
The University of Cambridge is founded	1209
The Magna Carta is signed by King John of England	1215
The Fifth Crusade begins	1217

BIBLIOGRAPHY

* Goldberg, Enia A., and Norman Itzkowitz. **Genghis Khan: 13th-Century Mongolian Tyrant**. New York: Franklin Watts, 2008.

Man, John. **Genghis Khan: Life, Death, and Resurrection**. New York: St. Martin's Press, 2004.

Ratchnevsky, Paul. **Genghis Khan: His Life and Legacy**. Translated and Edited by Thomas Nivison Haining. Oxford, UK, and Cambridge, Mass.: Basil Blackwell Ltd, 1991.

Robertson, Eliza. "**The Book That Waited: The Loss and Rediscovery of The Secret History of the Mongols**." *World Literature Today*, July 23, 2012.

Tanner, Stephen. **Afghanistan: A Military History from Alexander the Great to the War Against the Taliban**. Philadelphia: Da Capo Press, 2002.

Weatherford, Jack. **Genghis Khan and the Making of the Modern World**. New York: Crown Publishers, 2004.

* Books for young readers